THE LITTLE BOOK OF
GOLF TIPS

A practical guide to Golf

Written by Jeremy Ellwood

THE LITTLE BOOK OF
GOLF TIPS
A practical guide to Golf

This edition first published in the UK in 2008
By Green Umbrella Publishing

© Green Umbrella Publishing 2008

www.gupublishing.co.uk

Publishers Jules Gammond & Vanessa Gardner

Printed and bound in China

ISBN 978-1-905828-48-7

Introduction

Numerous books on golf technique have been written by those far more qualified than me, so this book will focus more on alternative, perhaps easier-to-achieve ways of improving than eliminating that flying right elbow or getting your left arm fully extended at the top. Experts say you should limit your swing thoughts to one – maybe two at a pinch – out on the course, so what good would it do anyway to fill your mind with countless technical "do's and don'ts" as you stand over the ball? Therein lies the path to the fabled but undesirable state of "paralysis by analysis".

Shooting the lowest possible score is about so much more than technique alone. It's also about thinking effectively on and off the course, adopting appropriate strategies, applying a liberal dose of common sense, and making sure your equipment is helping rather than hindering you.

You will find some technical tips within these pages, but they're mostly confined to those generally regarded as universal truths, steering clear of more complex notions that a) would be hard to explain and demonstrate in 100 words and b) might be wholly unworkable within the framework of your unique swing. Wise teaching pros would often rather refine what you already have than embark on major swing surgery that demands more time than most working folk can realistically give.

Most of the tips that follow require a little extra thought, not as you stand over the ball, but either before you do so, or before you even set foot on the course. Several are grounded in nothing more than common sense – but how often is that the first thing to go when trouble sets in?

This practical guide seeks to challenge your thinking and decision-making on the course, provide strategic advice to help you use every piece of available information to your potential advantage, and offer equipment-related tips that highlight how simple tweaks to your line-up might suddenly free you up to score.

My own swing is not a thing of great beauty and my 5-handicap game is built on the principle of "not how, but how many" rather than textbook technique. I would say that of the numerous tips and pointers I've picked up along the way, few of the ones that have really struck a chord would be classed as technical. Encouraging news for every golfer!

Jeremy Ellwood

1

Make sure your lay-ups really are lay-ups

Laying up short of water, cross-bunkers or other hazards right on your limit is very sensible. But things can go horribly wrong if you base club selection too closely on the exact yardage to the hazard's edge. Being free from the mental pressure of a specific target exacerbates the problem, as we often time our shots better then. It's little consolation to be able to say, "but I really flushed that!" as you reach for another ball to replace your submerged one. So when laying up, take at least one, maybe two clubs less than the distance to the hazard's edge.

2

Check pin positions whenever possible

Few courses provide daily pin position charts and with greens typically 25-40 yards long, the exact flag location can make two or three clubs' difference. It's often tricky to determine where the flag is as you eye up your approach, so whenever course geography takes you close to greens you've yet to play, make a mental or physical note of the pin positions. And remember, on tiered greens it may be more important to be on the right level than the putting surface itself, with a chip from just off the green usually easier than a putt up or down its full length.

3

Hit quick downhill putts out of the toe

You won't often be advised to try and deliberately mis-hit shots, but sometimes it's a shrewd option on slippery downhill putts. Using the toe of the club will mean the ball leaves the face of the putter less sharply, thus reducing the chances of it "going off in your hands". You'll be less prone to decelerating or jabbing at the ball, and less likely to suffer the three-putt consequences associated with such frowned-upon putting crimes.

4

Hit shots softer, not harder, into the wind

For many golfers, this simply doesn't make sense. If you're fighting a howling gale head on surely you need to hit the ball as hard as possible? But the harder you hit the ball the more spin you impart, and into the wind, more backspin means a greater chance of your ball ballooning and coming up way short, while any sidespin will be vastly exaggerated, potentially sending it miles off-line. So, hard though it may be to fully fathom, think controlled tempo rather than brute force into a headwind.

5
Keep your wrists out of simple chips

Many golfers believe they have to help the ball up on straightforward chips, breaking their wrists and scooping at it in an ill-advised attempt to get it airborne. Don't do this as it overcomplicates an essentially simple action, bringing all manner of horror shots needlessly into the equation. Wedges have up to 64° of loft – more than enough for virtually any scenario. So let the club do the lofting work and keep your wrists nice and firm through impact. You'll soon become a much more consistent chipper.

6
Check your alignment often

To improve your chances of hitting it where you're trying to, your feet, hips and shoulders should all be pointing at the target. If they're aiming too far left you're likely to cut the ball; too far right and you're likely to hook it. Check your feet by placing a club on the ground with the shaft touching both sets of toes, before stepping away to see where it's pointing. Hips and shoulders can be trickier, so if you can't work things out for yourself, ask a golfer whose opinion you respect, or find a driving range fitted out with all-revealing mirrors.

7

Sometimes it's best to play for the fat of the green

Since you're not blessed with Tiger's sublime shot-making skills, attacking dangerous pins can have serious repercussions for your score. So be sensible. If a pin is cut perilously close to water, deep bunkers or severe slopes, play for the fat of the green as par will invariably be easier from here than some greenside horror spot. It's demoralising to hit a perfect drive, attack unwisely and walk off with a big score when you'd been in position "A" just moments earlier. So don't fall for the "sucker pin" – bide your time and wait for more opportune moments to attack.

8

Putt whenever practically possible

Reaching for your lob wedge to play simple shots from just off the green is rarely the percentage play in any quest to shoot the lowest possible score – especially if you're an average chipper at best. Assuming the lie is not too thick or fluffy, your worst putt will almost always be better than your worst chip and often better than your best one. So putt whenever practically possible. If you're keen to develop your chip shot repertoire, do it on the practice ground where the odd duff or thin won't ruin an otherwise healthy scorecard.

9

Sometimes it's best to take a drop, even if you're tempted to play

If you're in trouble under bushes or in trees, don't feel compelled to try and play the ball as it lies. If your backswing catches on a branch, you could miss it altogether or hit it into even deeper trouble. When the potential downside outweighs the possible gains, don't be reluctant to take a drop, especially if that then leaves you clear to make a full swing. Take your medicine and move on. You'll undoubtedly reduce the number of big scores you run up, and will still be able to salvage par sometimes, even with the drop.

10

Hit the club YOU need to hit

Even though you can't ask other players what club they're using, you'll often have a pretty good idea, especially on par 3s. But even if you do, you should view this merely as "information of general interest" rather than letting it unduly sway your club selection. Your opponent or partner might be a club or two longer or shorter than you, or may see the shot very differently – perhaps a high draw with an 8-iron while you see it as a punched fade with a 5-iron. Whatever the case, hit the club you think you need to hit for the way you've seen the shot.

11
Don't flatter yourself!

Any pro will tell you that the single most common error amateurs make in pro-ams is not hitting enough club. Most golfers flatter themselves over their distances. They remember the one-in-twenty 7-iron they flushed 180 yards, overlooking that it was downhill, downwind and pitched 20 yards short before running up. They forget their 7-iron normally flies 140 yards, so invariably come up short where most of the trouble usually lies. So play to your normal limits rather than your personal best if you want to find the finely-mown grass more often.

12
Double-check whether yardages are to the front or middle of the green

Where courses afford you the luxury of yardages via course planners or sprinkler heads, make 100% sure that you know whether they're to the front or middle of the green, otherwise your approach shots will be out all round. If they're to the front it can be hard to get that figure out of your mind, so try and instinctively add 15 yards for a typical middle of the green distance. And on the continent don't forget to do the necessary conversion by adding 10% to any metric figures for a pretty accurate yardage equivalent.

13

Make sure your wedges have the right "sole bounce" for your game

The degree of bounce in the sole of a wedge – typically 6° to 16° – dictates how much the club is likely to bounce at impact. In low bounce wedges, the leading edge sits flusher to the ground – handy for getting to the bottom of the ball from tight lies or sparsely-filled bunkers. In high bounce wedges, the leading edge sits further from the ground – ideal for preventing the leading edge digging in too much from lush grass or well-filled bunkers. To ensure you always have a wedge for the job in hand, it's as important to have different bounce options at your disposal as different lofts.

14

Get yourself a gap wedge

Lofts on pitching wedges have been getting stronger over the years, while those on sand wedges have stayed roughly the same. Typically there might now be a 9° or 10° jump between the two (46/47° to 56°) – considerably more than one club's worth of distance difference. So if you're forever having to force your sand wedge or rein in your pitching wedge, get yourself a gap wedge. With lofts from 50° to 54°, they slot neatly in the middle, allowing you to make a normal swing from those awkward in-between distances.

15

Watch others putt

If you're not sure about the break or pace of a putt, observe closely all other putts on that green before yours – especially any of a similar line or distance. It will give you vital clues that could prevent you leaving yours short, blasting it miles past or getting the line totally wrong. You can't stand directly on another player's line either behind them or beyond the hole as they putt, and it would be poor etiquette to hover too closely. But there's always a point at which you can see clearly how a putt behaves without getting in the way.

16

Assess risky shots shrewdly

There always seems to be a little voice in our heads goading us in to going for risky shots, so it's wise to establish some sort of fixed rule to help rationalise the decision-making process. Annika Sorenstam famously employs a "6 out of 10" rule in which she will only go for shots she feels she's can pull off six times in every 10. Bearing in mind how much more gifted than us she is, an "8 out of 10" rule might be more appropriate for us – unless we're prepared to deal with the consequences if the shot doesn't come off.

17

Praise yourself for good shots to the same degree you rebuke yourself for bad ones

If you're prone to berating yourself over bad shots, do you also praise yourself to the same degree over good ones? Probably not, creating a one-sided mental relationship with your golf, and giving every bad shot free rein to herald the beginning of the end for your score. The laws of physics say that for each and every action there is an equal and opposite reaction, so why not adapt this to your golf and start praising your good shots to the same degree you beat yourself up over bad ones. You might even feel a little better for it.

18

Don't show your hand too soon in matchplay

Reaching for the club you intend to use too soon can give your opponent vital clues about your intentions, and influence his choice of play. If it's his honour and you stride to the tee armed only with your driver, you've blown your cover and he may well adapt his strategy accordingly – perhaps just hitting an iron to get it in play. Better to keep him guessing, force him to make the choice and only draw your weapon when it's your turn to play. Uncertainty or niggling doubt could mean he doesn't commit fully to the shot, leaving you the chance to play safely for the win.

19

Statistics don't have to be one step on from damned lies!

Do you know for sure which areas of your game need most work? Keeping detailed stats can clarify things. For example, is it poor putting or inaccurate approach play that's causing a birdie drought or glut of three-putts? Assuming one when it's really the other could leave you focusing on the wrong things in practice. So why not keep a record of stats like fairways hit, greens in regulation, distances from the pin or putts per round. It may confirm what you already know, but equally could highlight what you hadn't realised or perhaps didn't want to face up to.

20

Make sure you're playing with the right shaft flex

Club-fitting is now widely available so there's no excuse for any reasonably serious golfer to be playing with the wrong shafts. The correct flex depends on your unique launch conditions, based around factors such as clubhead speed, ball speed and angle of attack. Shafts that are too stiff will tend to fly low and right while those that are too flexible will err high and left, or generate a random shot dispersion. Seek expert advice and make sure the shafts in your clubs are helping you perform to your potential rather than holding you back.

21

Pace is more critical than line on long-range putts

Far more second putts are missed because of shortcomings in the first putt's length than its line. On a reasonably flat green, if you get the pace about right you'd have to be way out on line to leave yourself more than three feet away. So when weighing up a putt, make sure you spend adequate time gauging the required strength before taking the putter back, rather than getting bogged down on line alone. Honing your long-range distance control will mean far fewer three-putts.

22

Set your "mark and wait" threshold on the greens, then stick to it!

Only you will know exactly what length putt constitutes an unmissable tap-in for you and what length you'd rather mark and wait. The important thing is that whenever a putt extends beyond your "mark and wait" threshold, that is exactly what you must do – mark and wait. More apparent "gimmes" are missed through breaking this routine out of frustration or complacency than any other cause. The scorecard sees no difference between 300 yards and two feet and the game is tough enough anyway without carelessly throwing shots away!

23

Check wind direction in a clear spot

Usually the wind blows from a fairly constant direction throughout a typical round but it can be hard to gauge on tree-lined courses where it swirls or hides at ground level or in tucked-away corners. So find a clear spot to check the general wind direction and if necessary cross-reference it against a course map so you can better judge things on later holes when it's less obvious. If in doubt, go with this general wind direction unless there's strong evidence to suggest it swirls in a particular part of the course.

24

Keep your clubfaces clean

Pros never hit a shot without making sure clubfaces and grooves are free from mud, grass and water. Many of us are rather less meticulous. Of course, they have the luxury of a caddy, but a few seconds with a towel and one of those handy little groove-cleaning brushes – or even a tee-peg – is not that onerous. Dirty faces and grooves could be costing you shots as they deprive you of clean contact and maximum control. Don't neglect the driver either, especially if its face has no central scorelines – trapping water between face and ball at impact can affect flight and distance.

25

Use the markings on your ball to help you line up putts

Fewer things offer more scope for ready-made visual assistance than the markings on your ball. Many golfers find it helpful to align the ball's brand or model name to the line of their putts, then set their putter face at right angles to this marking. Some balls even have arrows stamped on for this very purpose. But if you change your mind once you've placed your ball, it's vital that you stop, remark and adjust to reap the full benefits of this perfectly legal little trick.

26

Tighten forearm muscles for a cleaner strike from fairway bunkers

Clean contact can be difficult on long bunker shots, yet one simple adjustment could help you strike the ball crisply more often. Very rarely will anyone tell you to tighten your muscles in golf as it's a game best played free of tension. But tensing your forearm muscles just a fraction shortens them a little thus reducing the risk of you taking too much sand and your ball flying only a fraction of the desired distance. Don't overdo it though, and do make sure it's only your forearm muscles.

27

Invest in one or more utility or hybrid clubs

The longest irons pose a tough test for all golfers, especially off the deck. Thankfully, there's now a more playable alternative in the utility, hybrid or rescue club. Most golfers will find it far easier to launch long-range missiles with these compact-headed mini-woods than their unyielding long iron counterparts. And from certain grades of rough the contest is a no-brainer with the utility club bringing greens back into range that long irons can't even contemplate. So if you haven't yet got one, invest without further delay and join the scores of top pros ditching their longest irons.

28

Use your handicap sensibly

Handicaps allow players of lesser ability to compete on equal terms by granting them extra shots on certain holes. Sometimes it may be best to "use" your shot on a particularly tough hole and look to make up ground elsewhere. So if there's a 450-yard par-4 "shot hole" you can't even sniff in two, why thrash away wildly in a futile attempt to do just that with all the inherent risk? Play three safe shots and move on to better opportunities. You'll run up fewer big numbers, and will of course still sometimes get up and down for par.

29

Coping with sidehill lies

Sidehill lies demand adjustments to your set-up. If the ball is below your feet, keep more weight on your heels to stop you falling forwards, grip the club at the very top and allow for a fade as your swing plane will be steeper than usual. If the ball is above your feet, keep your weight more towards your toes to stop you toppling backwards, choke down on the grip and allow for a draw or hook as your swing plane becomes flatter. Focus on a smooth tempo too, as the harder you swing the more likely you are to fall off balance.

30

Open the clubface before taking your grip on greenside splash shots

You probably know to play the majority of your greenside bunker shots from an open stance with an open clubface to help you cut across the ball and pop it out. But there are big "dos" and "don'ts". Do set the club open by the required amount before taking your grip; don't take your stance and then from this position twist the club face open as you'll be tweaking your hands into too strong a position – just what you don't want in a bunker.

31
Restrict release to hit the ball lower

Lower shots that are less susceptible to strong gusts are advisable when playing in headwinds or crosswinds. Restricting your hand release through impact will reduce the club's effective loft and send the ball away on a more boring trajectory. It's a little like an extended chip and run, where you're always looking to keep the wrists fairly passive. So why not start off practising greenside chip-and-runs, then gradually work your way back, trying to retain that feeling of limited release compared to a normal swing.

32
Try the "funnel approach" as you walk down to a ball in potential trouble

Your mind can run rampant when you've just hit your ball offline, conjuring up all manner of imagined lies and worst case scenarios. But it's often hard to see what the damage really is, and since what's done is done anyway, why not switch off and think about something else on the walk down. Then, over the last 20 or so yards, "funnel" your concentration back in once you've got a clearer idea about the shot you now face. Your fears may prove unfounded and it will stop you getting unnecessarily down on yourself.

33

Learn to read your divots

Use your divots' diagnostic properties to guide your practice, and seek professional help if you can't remedy things on your own. Excessively deep divots mean you're attacking the ball too steeply, often resulting in heavy contact, while shallow or barely visible divots suggest too shallow an attack and a greater risk of thin contact. As for direction, if the divot points left of target, your swing is too much outside-to-in resulting in a fade or cut, and if it points right, your swing is too much inside-to-out with a draw or hook the most likely outcome.

34

Tee modern drivers up nice and high

Driver head sizes have grown exponentially in recent years, meaning the sweetspot now sits further from the ground. But we haven't all caught up yet in terms of teeing height, with most of us now needing to tee up a little or a lot higher than we once did to find the most effective part of the clubface. Too low a tee also increases the risk of you consciously or sub-consciously cutting across the ball to try and help it into the air, so a higher tee could also see more of your drives ending up on the short grass.

35

Make sure your glove fits properly

Better to play with no glove at all than an ill-fitting one. Playing with too large a glove is an all too common crime, as is not replacing a sloppy, worn-out glove soon enough. In either scenario, unwanted "play" across the palm and in the fingers, deprives you of maximum grip as you swing. You'll reap optimum benefit if your glove fits like a second skin as it's intended to. If your scores matter to you, trying to squeeze every last drop out of a tired old glove is a false economy for the sake of a tenner!

36

Mentally rehearse shots by visualising what you want to do

Top players have long been using visualisation as a kind of pre-shot mental rehearsal, but it's something everyone can explore. You can picture yourself hitting the shot either through the eyes of an external observer or your own. Why not try storing away in your mind specific occasions when you've executed perfect shots with each club, then recalling as vivid an image in your mind as possible of how that looked and felt next time you face a similar shot with the same club?

37

Remember golf is supposed to be fun

For most of us, golf is a hobby, which my dictionary defines as "an enjoyable activity engaged in for pleasure and relaxation during spare time". In other words, it should be fun, and while it's never that much fun when we're playing really badly, some of us look far too miserable for it to make any sense in us being out on the course at all. So if the game's all getting too much, why not step away from the course for a while to evaluate things and seek ways to resolve them. Golf should never be a chore.

38

Stay in the present and take it one shot at a time

The next shot alone should command your complete focus. If your mind's forever harking back to mistakes just made, or racing ahead to tough holes yet to come, you're not giving your next shot its full due attention. The only thing you have real control over is the next shot you face and your chances of success increase significantly if it occupies all your thoughts. So stay in the present even if you have to use a trigger word like "stop" to drag yourself back to it.

39

Let go of bad shots

We all have different ways of reacting to bad shots. Some shout, swear and maybe even throw the odd club; others fume away silently to themselves. Either way, if you're still mulling that bad shot over as you stand over the next one, you're on a one-way trip to scorecard oblivion. We've all played with people who've let bad shots turn promising rounds into disasters, so know how damaging it can be to dwell on them. So after the initial reaction, let it go and move on. It's the only way to prevent one bad shot derailing an otherwise good round.

40

Don't hit until all doubt is eliminated

There's a lot to factor into every shot before deciding which club to hit. Where's the wind? How firmly or softly is it likely to land? Is it playing one or two clubs uphill? But problems arise if we're still deliberating as we take the club away, rather than making a firm decision then totally committing to the shot. Even if we're wrong, a committed swing often leads to less trouble than one in which you've suddenly decided halfway down you've got too much club or have misjudged the wind. So never start your swing until all doubt has been eliminated.

41

Learn golf's "get out of jail" wrong-handed shots

Sometimes your ball will end up where a right-hander has no shot but a left-hander would be fine – the wrong side of a tree or up against a hedge. Being able to advance the ball even a short distance may sometimes make the next shot easier or bring the green back into range. So experiment with improvised wrong-handed shots in practice, either by turning the clubhead round and hitting the ball with the toe, or by turning your back to the line of play and playing one-handed. Both could save you a shot or two every now and then – but always proceed cautiously and realistically.

42

Accept that others may just have played better than you

Golfers tend to get unduly bogged down in results, often automatically associating defeat with bad play. This doesn't always follow and it may be that although you played well, someone else just played that little bit better. You can't control this. You can only control what you do, so why jump to illogical conclusions about the way you've just played? It could leave you feeling unduly down, or considering working on things that simply don't need working on.

43

Get yourself custom-fitted

Do you know for sure that the 14 clubs in your bag are the best specification and line-up for your swing, or have you just bought off the shelf or inherited someone else's cast-offs that may be totally inappropriate for the way you play? All major brands now offer a variety of comprehensive fitting options, so book yourself a session to pinpoint the right line-up to help you get the most out of your game and ensure you're not throwing away needless shots through ill-suited clubs.

44

Reduce driver slice without overhauling your swing

If you're among the golfing majority fighting a slice rather than a hook with the driver, you may be able to reduce its severity without rebuilding your swing. Firstly, try an offset model in which the face sits slightly behind the shaft line giving you a fraction longer to square things at impact. Secondly, try a driver with an in-built draw bias courtesy of extra weight near the heel. Finally, try a higher loft, as lower lofts will exaggerate any sidespin. If none of these help, accept and allow for your slice, or undergo swing surgery with your pro.

45

Practise with feet together to improve balance and strike

If your ball-striking has gone off the boil, practising with your feet together could help get things back on track. It will eliminate any unwanted swaying and force you to refocus on rhythm and tempo, as you'll simply topple over if you swing too hard. It can also help you release the club properly at impact, as you really have no option but to do so if you want to remain upright. This exercise can often quickly improve your rhythm and striking – and you'll probably surprise yourself just how far you can still hit it.

46

Dealing with awkward left-to-right winds

Most right-handed golfers find left-to-right winds the hardest to cope with, especially off the tee. This is because more golfers hit a fade or slice than a draw or hook – a flight shape that left-to-right winds will only exaggerate. The best option is not to fight the wind too hard as it's easy to overcompensate and end up hooking it. Simply turn the toe of your club in a fraction at address, then make a normal smooth swing. This simple step should hold the ball against the wind enough to keep it safely in play.

47

Pick a spot on the ground just ahead of the ball to swing over

To help you stay down through the ball and swing through on line, concentrate on something a few inches in front of your ball on the line you want your club to pass over after impact – maybe a distinctive blade of grass or a bare patch. It should prevent you coming up out of the shot too early. If shots have been leaking one way or the other you may be able to straighten things up by making the mark just outside the line if you've been cutting the ball, or just inside it if you've been hooking.

48

Don't take on high-tariff shots without practice

Certain high-board dives attract higher tariffs than others because they're technically more complex. But while no diver would attempt one without hours of practice, we're all too eager to take on high-tariff golf shots we've never tried before and have little idea how to play. So next time you're contemplating curving the ball round trees or punching it under branches, stop and ask yourself, "do I know how to do this?" If not, go for a safer option and log it down as one to practise or seek expert advice about. It's the best way to avoid making bad situations worse.

49

Don't judge performance purely by results

We live in a result-driven society so it's no surprise many of us judge our golf on results alone, which opens the door to frequent failure. Results are important, but not the be-all-and-end-all. When we play well but things just don't happen, we need to ask, "did I play the way I set out to play and stick to the tasks I'd set myself?" If the answer is "yes", then be patient and trust that the results will come. When you've done everything you'd set out to do, reacting purely to results can leave you feeling unnecessarily down. So focus more on how you played than what you scored when assessing performance.

50

"One ball practice" can sharpen up your game

If all your friendly games are too far removed from the competition environment it can be quite a shock when every shot counts and every putt must be holed. There are no Mulligans and few "gimmes" in competitive golf, so to emulate the real thing more closely, devote some practice to "one ball golf". It's relatively easy to hole a putt, or chip your ball close at the second time of asking when you've seen how the first one behaves. But one chance is all you get when the gun goes off, and a spot of "one ball practice" will give your game a sharper edge.

51

Don't be too hasty to play out sideways

It's wise to take your medicine when you've found a spot of bother, but some golfers definitely exceed the dosage. Weigh up all your options before automatically chipping out sideways. Is there a marginally riskier play that could gain you 40 or 50 yards? Could you lob it over that bush or thread it through those trees reasonably safely? If not, come out sideways. But if so, every yard closer to the green could minimise the damage as I'm sure you find more greens from 150 yards than 200? So assess things fully before playing at right angles.

52

Learn the utility or wood chip

From certain greenside lies, precise controlled contact can be tricky with wedges or irons – perhaps when you're up against the collar or in a slightly fluffy lie. Chipping with a utility club or fairway wood could be the answer, as their larger, contoured soles are more forgiving and much less likely to snag. You'll need to practise this shot, as the ball does come off the clubface quite quickly. And because these clubs are longer than wedges or irons, you may need to grip down onto the shaft to retain control and get the sole sitting properly.

53

Make sure your stance is not too wide

Many golfers lean towards too wide a stance, perhaps in the belief that it enhances their stability as they swing. Actually, it makes it more difficult to turn and transfer weight properly, leading to excessive use of the upper body and arms. For the longer clubs, your feet should be wide enough apart to maintain your balance but no wider than shoulder width, getting progressively narrower in the shorter irons. This will mean your lower body and legs can create power more effectively via proper weight transfer and rotation.

54

Try shorter putters before belly or broomhandle models

If putting woes persist, try a shorter putter first before entering the world of belly or broomhandle models. The latter take more time to master than most golfers can spare, while shorter putters allow arms to hang more freely, which automatically relieves some of the wrist and arm tension that can hamper attempts at a smooth takeaway and stroke. David Howell uses a 32in putter – two or three inches shorter than standard – despite being over 6ft tall.

55

A ball is not just a ball

Dismissing all golf balls as the same could be costing you shots. Their more subtle spin and trajectory differences may be hard to distinguish, but you can easily tell how hard or soft a ball is. Switching from one to the other will make things a bit of a lottery – especially on and around the greens. So for consistency, find a ball you like and stick with it. If you're not sure about one you've just found, bounce it off your putter or do the fingernail test, then consign any that are either too hard or too soft to the practice ball bag. This could save you more shots than you realise.

56

Get your eyes directly over the ball to see a putt's true line

Putting is far from a precise science with countless top players adopting highly idiosyncratic styles over the years to great effect. However, if your putter's been underperforming – especially on the direction front – check whether the line from your eyes to the ball at address is perpendicular to the ground or at a slight angle. If it's the latter, try re-aligning your eyes so they're directly over the ball at address. Many experts believe this provides the most accurate view of a putt's line, free from potentially confounding angles.

57

Try and find something good in every round

More golfers dwell on the negatives than the positives. But just as it's good to try and see the best in other people, so too is it better to find the positives in every round, even if it's just one shot that came off perfectly or simply the realisation that you now know what you need to go away and work on. Often, things aren't as bad as you think, and even if they are, dwelling on them isn't going to help. So, without deluding yourself, try to become a "half-full" rather than a "half-empty" golfer, however much that goes against the grain.

58

Adjust your stance for simple chips

Set-up should be very different for greenside chips than for full shots, as chips require no weight transfer and are best played with the lower body relatively inactive. The best way to achieve this is to narrow your stance significantly, with feet slightly open to the target, weight favouring the left side and hands slightly ahead of the ball. The idea then is to emulate your putting stroke more than your golf swing, with backswing and follow-through roughly the same length. Using your normal stance and action overcomplicates an essentially straightforward movement.

59

Read more borrow into hard-breaking putts

More golfers read too little into cross-slope putts than too much, typically missing on the low side. This means the ball is working away from the hole as it dies, potentially leaving you much still to ponder. Overborrowing, on the other hand, is often referred to as "missing on the pro's side". Why? Because pros know how treacherous cross-slope putts are, and by erring on the high side the ball will be working towards the hole rather than away from it as it dies. So remember, there's probably more break than you imagine, and overborrowing leads to fewer three-putts.

60

Don't forget to read your chips

Knowing you've hit a chip exactly as intended only for your ball to be swept offline by an unseen slope can be immensely frustrating. While most of us devote plenty of time to reading putts, we often neglect to do likewise from off the green, even though a typical chip spends more time rolling like a putt than flying through the air. So spend time working out how the ball is going to roll on landing to prevent the potential fruits of a perfectly executed chip being wasted just because you neglected to fully survey the lie of the land.

61

Practise tough chips to improve your up-and-down success rate

For many of us, chipping practice consists of a few shots from carefully-selected lies just off the edge of a flat bit of green with no obstacles in our way. Sadly, out on the course, our balls tend to find considerably more awkward and challenging lies. So to improve your up-and-down percentage, broaden your chipping practice to include bad lies, awkward slopes, shots over bunkers or mounds, and delicate chips to tight pins. It will improve your creativity and help you make a better fist of things from similar lies out on the course.

62

You don't have to keep your head regimentally still

Every golfer will at some time have been told to keep his head still. But is it true? Yes – as long as you don't take it too literally. If your head sways significantly as you take the club away it probably means you're not turning properly, and if it's up looking for the ball long before contact then disaster will follow. But keeping it rigidly still introduces unnecessary tension into a fluid movement. So do focus on the ball until after impact, but don't fight the natural little movements your head wants to make. Keeping it stock still turns a fluid movement into a wooden one – and few wooden golfers succeed.

63

If in doubt opt for the longer club

Watch golfers playing into any green in normal conditions and you'll see far more balls coming up short than hurtling through the back. Why? Because we tend to base club selection on personal bests rather than averages, fail to allow enough for wind or slope or forget that most greens are 30 to 40 yards long. But with trouble more often at the front than the back, missing long is usually the preferable option. So, other than in a strong tailwind, take the longer club when in doubt. You'll end up putting far more often, and find less greenside trouble.

64

A good swing starts with a good grip

For most golfers, the grip – or "hold" as some pros now call it because it implies less pressure – should be "neutral". You should be able to see two to two and a half knuckles of your upper hand at address, with the lines formed between thumbs and index fingers pointing towards your right shoulder. If more knuckles are visible, your grip is too strong and a hook the most likely result; fewer knuckles and your grip is too weak, probably resulting in a fade or slice that lacks power and distance. Get your grip right, and everything that follows has more chance of falling into place.

65

Shaping shots is not as hard as you think

Shaping shots intentionally is more straightforward than many think. Point your feet, shoulders and hips in the direction you want the ball to start, and your clubface at the target so it will appear either closed for a draw or open for a fade. Do this before taking your grip. When everything is set, commit fully to the shot and resist any subconscious urge to twist the clubface back to square through impact. But always temper ambition with prudence, and don't attempt shot-shaping beyond the laws of physics.

66

Revert to simple shots to regain confidence

If confidence has flown the nest there's no point endlessly practising the very shots that have drained you of it. Why not revert to something so easy you can't help but succeed just to kick-start things again? If it's ages since you holed a putt, hit a couple of dozen from an "unmissable" distance – a foot, two feet, whatever – just to see the ball disappear with all the associated sound effects. Or if your iron striking has gone off the boil, practise off a tee-peg for a while so you get to see the ball soaring away. It could just trigger a revival in both confidence and form.

67

Keep your tempo the same back and through

Tempo is critical, but there is no universal standard. Ernie Els, Retief Goosen and Fred Couples have languid, effortless-looking swings; others like Nick Price, Greg Norman and Ian Poulter have quicker, more purposeful tempos. The key is not how hard you appear to be swinging, but whether or not the pace of your swing is the same on the way back as it is through the ball. Problems arise when the backswing gets out of sync with the down swing, so try to keep the two evenly matched.

68

Vary backswing length to control pitching distance

What happens when you face a less-than-full-distance pitch? How do you hit the ball just 75 or 50 yards? Too many of us are guilty of making a full backswing, then decelerating on the way down in an ill-advised attempt to shave off the necessary yards. The simplest way is to keep tempo the same, but reduce the length of your backswing – for example perhaps a ¾ length backswing for 75 yards or a ½ backswing for 50 yards. It takes practice, but is the most effective and reliable way to control less-than-full pitches.

69

Don't panic if your ball's in a divot

Finding yourself in a deepish divot after a perfect drive is hugely frustrating, but it's far better to accept and deal with it than stand there bemoaning your ill-fortune. The laws of physics dictate that you'll need to make certain adjustments if you're to get to the bottom of the ball, so move it back in your stance, then drive down on it more steeply than usual with a firm committed swing. You may or may not retain a degree of control, but from all but the deepest of divots you should still be able to advance the ball pretty much the desired distance.

70

Learn the belly wedge

You may have tapped in the odd six-incher using your wedge's leading edge, but it's also very much a percentage shot when you need to take potentially damaging ground contact out of the equation – up against the collar round the green where fringe becomes rough, or on a downslope of shortish grass where it's all too easy to stub the shot. Use your putting stroke and try and make contact halfway up the ball. It's not as hard as you think and can be a real shot-saver when all other options carry far greater risks.

71

Play the hole from the green backwards to improve strategy

Have you ever tried playing holes from green to tee – either physically (but without the ball), or in your mind? It's a great way of pinpointing where you want to place your tee-shot for the best route in. Is the approach easier from the left or right? Does the green slope away so that it will be easier to control a full wedge than a pitch on short par-4s, making hanging back off the tee a more sensible option than attacking? Looking back up a hole can help you form more educated strategies in these and other scenarios.

72

Replace worn-out grips as soon as they need replacing

Trying to extend grip life beyond its working limit is a false economy, especially in winter when hands tend to get colder and drier. Grip life can be optimised by washing in warm soapy water and roughing them up a little with a file or sand paper. But eventually the only solution is to replace them, as slippery worn-out grips make you hold on too tightly, creating tension in the hands, wrists and arms that will stop you releasing the club properly even if you do manage to hold onto it. So never exceed a grip's natural working life.

73

Gear up for wet weather golf

Scores on soggy days are invariably higher than usual because eventually there comes a point where you just can't keep hold of the club. A caddy is the best answer – but few of us enjoy such luxury. So if you want the sun to shine on your game while it pours on others, the two most important things are extra towels in carrier bags or any dry pockets your bag possesses, and special wet weather gloves (don't be embarrassed to wear a pair), the best of which really do work. A healthy degree of patience and a sense of humour will also help – if at all possible!

74

Grip pressure is very important

How firmly do you hold the club? Are you a "death grip" merchant unwittingly strangling the life out of your club and probably your score? Or is your grip so light you're prone to losing control of the club at key stages of the swing? Those more qualified than me have likened optimum grip pressure to holding a small bird – too loose and it will fly away through your fingers; too tight and you risk crushing it. If that mental image doesn't do the trick, imagine ideal grip pressure to be just over halfway along a line from "very loose" to "very tight" (i.e. perhaps 5½ or 6 out of 10).

75

Play bunker-style splash shots from fluffy or lush greenside lies

We've all faced shots from grassy greenside lies that we're not quite sure how to tackle. Too cute with a chip-style shot and the most likely result is a stalling dribble as grass stops club in its tracks, leaving you facing the same shot again. Far better to generate the necessary clubhead speed to eliminate the risk of snagging by playing a positive bunker-style splash shot. Open the face, and focus on hitting the grass an inch or two behind the ball. You'll have a better chance of your ball popping out nicely and landing softly. It requires practice, but will leave you putting more often.

76

Only do what you have to do on the greens in matchplay

If you're 30 feet away in two while your opponent is 20 feet away in three in matchplay, there's little point being needlessly aggressive with your first putt. Yes, if you make it you've won the hole outright. But more often than not, two-putting will also win you the hole. So without becoming negative, concentrate all your efforts on getting your first putt within "gimme" distance to leave your opponent facing the tricky task of having to hole from 20 feet for the half.

77

Maximise fairway width off the tee

Most golfers hit the ball left-to-right or right-to-left off the tee rather than dead straight. If your flight shape is pretty consistent, you can maximise fairway width on many holes by teeing up close to the right-hand tee markers if you fade or left-hand markers if you draw, then aiming for the left or right half of the fairway respectively. With your normal flight you'll end up in the middle, but if you hit one straight or your shot shape becomes exaggerated, you will have increased your chances of staying on the fairway or in the first cut.

78

Better to play with what you've got on a given day

Sometimes, for any number of reasons, your usual shot shape eludes you or your yardages seem to be a little down – perhaps as a result of a bad back or your set-up being a fraction out. It's far wiser on these occasions to accept and play with what you've got on a given day than to constantly strive for your usual game. So play with the shape and distances you've been dealt, then evaluate and address the root causes after the round rather than during it. You will almost certainly score better on the day.

79
Maintain a healthy right knee flex throughout your backswing
One of the best ways to ensure your hips turn rather than slide on your backswing is to concentrate on maintaining your right knee flex as you take the club away. This makes it far easier for your hips to turn or rotate, thus creating power. Locking your right knee on your backswing means you simply can't turn your hips fully as they will naturally slide and sway away from the ball, depriving you of any real power. Try it and see – then focus on maintaining sufficient right knee flex for your hips to turn against on the backswing.

80
Always use a tee-peg
Don't spurn the benefits of a tee unless you're a highly accomplished player – and even then many an expert would strongly discourage it because it's simply easier to hit the ball cleanly off a tee than the ground. Yes, good ball-strikers could argue that playing off the deck generates more spin and control on par-3s as you trap the ball between clubface and turf. But over the course of a season you'll save more shots simply by striking the ball cleanly more often.

81

Don't be too greedy from the toughest of bunker lies

Want to avoid those embarrassing Hamlet moments in which plenty of sand comes flying out of the bunker, while your ball remains firmly trapped? Then accept that there may be times when forward progress is simply out of the question. If your ball lies too close to a steep face, too near the back edge or inside the bunker while your feet are outside, come out sideways, backwards or any way that denies that particular bunker the pleasure of costing you more than one shot.

82

Practise with the ball above your feet if you're hitting shots heavy

If you're hitting a lot of heavy shots, your swing plane is probably out, causing you to come down into the ball too steeply. One way to work on this is to practise shots with the ball above your feet. You might think that this would encourage you to make even heavier contact as the ball will be closer to you at address. But actually it forces you to flatten out your swing plane – a feeling you can then take away and try to reproduce when you go back to hitting balls from normal lies.

Also available:

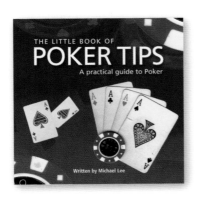

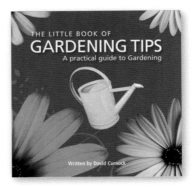

Available from all major stockists

The pictures in this book were provided courtesy of

GETTY IMAGES
www.gettyimages.com

SHUTTERSTOCK IMAGES
www.shutterstock.com

Design and artwork by David Wildish

Image research by Ellie Charleston

Creative Director: Kevin Gardner

Published by Green Umbrella Publishing

Publishers: Jules Gammond, Vanessa Gardner

Written by Jeremy Ellwood